IMPRESSIONS *of*
SCOTLAND

Produced by AA Publishing

© AA Media Ltd 2006

All rights reserved. No part of this publication may be reproduced, stored in
a retrieval system, or transmitted in any form or by any means – electronic,
photocopying, recording or otherwise – unless the written permission of the
publishers has been obtained beforehand.

Published by AA Publishing (a trading name of AA Media Ltd, whose registered
office is Fanum House, Basing View, Basingstoke, Hampshire RG21 4EA;
registered number 06112600)

Reprinted July 2009

ISBN-10: 0 7495 4861 4
ISBN-13: 978 0 7495 4861 2
A04179

A CIP catalogue record for this book is available from the British Library.
The contents of this book are believed correct at the time of printing. Nevertheless,
the publishers cannot be held responsible for any errors, omissions or for changes in
the details given in this book or for the consequences of any reliance on the
information provided by the same. This does not affect your statutory rights.

Printed by C&C Offset Printing, China

*Front cover: view of the River Ba towards
Black Mount, Rannoch Moor, Highlands.*

IMPRESSIONS *of*
SCOTLAND

Picture Acknowledgements

All photographs are held in the Automobile Association's own photo library (AA World Travel Library) and
were taken by the following photographers:

Marius Alexander 39, 70; Sue Anderson 28, 31, 76; Adrian Baker 44; Jeff Beazley 14, 27, 67, 90; Jim Carnie
35; Steve Day 10, 11, 16, 19, 36, 43, 51, 64, 66, 69, 71, 74, 78, 89, 91; Eric Ellington 57, 65; Richard Elliott
24, 45, 47, 55, 68, 79, 82, 84; Derek Forss 81; Stephen Gibson 25, 92; Jim Henderson 20, 22, 23, 26, 38, 42,
46, 62, 80; Anthony Hopkins 8; Ken Paterson 5, 37, 40, 41, 49, 52, 94; Peter Sharpe 60; Jonathan Smith 3, 33,
73, 83; Michael Taylor 12, 72; Stephen Whitehorn 7, 9, 13, 15, 17, 18, 29, 30, 32, 34, 53, 54, 56, 58, 59, 61, 63,
75, 77, 85, 86, 87, 88, 94; Ronnie Weir 21, 48, 50.

Opposite: Looking over Edinburgh's Old Town from Calton Hill.

INTRODUCTION

Scotland sells itself to the world as a land of misty mountains and big scenery, romantic and tragic history, tartan McHaggisry with a beating Celtic heart. Anybody who comes to these shores looking for this image is unlikely to leave disappointed – the mountains are undoubtedly majestic, the history rich and well told, and yes, some Scotsmen wear kilts.

But of course, Scotland has a great deal to offer beyond the clichés, as anyone who scratches the surface of this intriguing and contradictory land will soon discover. And it is the little personal discoveries – a glimpse of a hidden fairytale castle between the trees, the heady scent of a heather moor on a hot day, the unexpected sight of an otter nosing along the shore, a cheery conversation with the only other walkers on a bare mountainside, a fresh-washed beach of pure shell sand in a turquoise bay, a superb meal of fresh seafood in a pub you've chanced upon in a place where you can't begin to pronounce the Gaelic name – which make any visit here memorable. *Impressions of Scotland* reflects in superb photography the very best of the known and the less familiar in this remarkable north British land.

The Scottish determination to retain an identity separate from England remains strong, despite being politically joined since 1603. It's an identity reinforced by its own parliament, held in the historic capital of Edinburgh, a city built on hills and dominated by its famous castle. Edinburgh is the heart of Scotland's central belt – a land of battles and medieval splendour, of intellectual sophistication, of ancient trade routes, and of fishing and farming, with rugged castles and picturesque fishing villages contrasting with the 19th-century industrial tenements of Dundee. To the west,

Glasgow – Scotland's confident second city – has become known for its first-class shopping and superb museums and galleries, as shipbuilding and other heavy engineering have given way to a vibrant arts and entertainments scene. Part of the city's charm is that the hills, forests and beautiful countryside around Loch Lomond and the Trossachs are so accessible, with the scenic peninsulas of Argyll spilling west and south.

To the south the border country is a haven of peace and tranquillity, with quiet roads and lush pastures. Medieval abbeys, stately homes and small, stone-built towns are tucked into the folds of the rolling hills. Galloway and the Solway Coast are Scotland's best-kept secret, with endless miles of deserted sandy beaches, rocky coves and clifftop paths.

From Space, Scotland north of the Forth and Clyde looks like a loosely woven cloth – an ancient tartan perhaps – ragged at its western edge and crumpled in a series of irregular folds with loose scraps and threads around its fringes. These are the Highlands and Islands, characterised by high mountains and deep glens, tumbling rivers and shimmering lochs, open moors and spreading forests.

The far northern islands of Orkney are a handful of emeralds cast on the waters, their gentle green, undulating landscape in sharp contrast to the rocky islands of Shetland, slashed by the sea into thousands of inlets.

The Glasgow Science Centre – a gleaming three-storey titanium wonderland beside the River Clyde.

Abandoned fishing boats at Salen, on the Isle of Mull.
Opposite: Beinn Edra and the Trotternish Ridge on the Isle of Skye. The ridge is a 20-mile-long (32-km)
inland cliff winding down the middle of the Trotternish Peninsula.

Kenmore church dominates the town square on the banks of Loch Tay, Perthshire.

Steam trains cross the Glenfinnan Viaduct at the northeastern end of Loch Sheil. The viaduct, comprising 21 arches, is part of the Fort William to Mallaig extension of the West Highland Railway.

On the shore of Spey Bay, north of Fochabers, Grampian. The village is a base for the salmon-netting industry.
Opposite: Tobermory Harbour on the Isle of Mull.

Edinburgh Castle has dominated the capital city from its crag, Castle Rock, for eight centuries.
It has served as a royal palace, a military garrison and a battleground; today is it is Scotland's
prime tourist attraction.

The ruins of Kilchurn Castle stand at the head of Loch Awe, in Argyll.

Highland cattle, an ancient Scottish breed, roam free in the north of the country.
They come in a variety of colours, although reddish-brown is the most commonly seen.

The Cuillin Hills, looking across Loch Scavaig from Elgol, on Skye. This is the steepest mountain range in Britain, with more than 20 Munros – peaks over 3,000ft (914m).

The futuristic Glasgow Science Centre and the Glasgow Tower, Scotland's tallest freestanding structure.
Opposite: the view of Loch Tummel from the visitor centre at Queen's View, near Pitlochry, Tayside.

The dramatic ruins of medieval Dunnottar Castle occupy an isolated promontory rising above the North Sea near Stonehaven, in Aberdeenshire.

Montrose on the east coast is a royal burgh with a natural harbour on the River Esk. The tidal basin is an important wildfowl wintering area.

Lochs, moorland and mountains make up Glen Affric, north of Inverness, which also has one of the largest stands of ancient Caledonian pinewood remaining in Scotland.

Edzell Castle, near Brechin in Angus. It dates from the 16th century, when the original medieval tower house was incorporated into a courtyard mansion. The walled garden was added in 1604.

Erected in 1910, the Pencil Monument in Largs, north Ayrshire, commemorates a victory by the Scots over the Norwegians in 1263.

Opposite: Ben Chonzie, above Loch Turret in Perthshire. Its name is derived from the Gaelic for 'hill of moss'.

Thurso, mainland Britain's most northerly town at the northwest tip of Scotland. Its oldest part is Fishertown (above), with the ruins of Old St Peter's Kirk.

Balmoral Castle, in Aberdeenshire. It was completed in 1855 for Queen Victoria and is still used regularly by the royal family.

Black Mount – a range of mountains stretching from Glen Orchy to Glen Coe – and Rannoch Moor.

The Callanish Standing Stones on the Isle of Lewis. Until the mid-19th century the 50 or so boulders, which stand up to 15ft (3m) high and are arranged in a cruciform layout, were buried beneath several feet of peat.

Dun Carloway Broch on Lewis is one of the best-preserved prehistoric stone towers in Scotland.
Opposite: Rannoch Moor, a huge upland area of bog, rock and moorland on the edge of Glen Coe.

The Quiraing is one of the strange rock formations on the Trotternish Peninsula, on the Isle of Skye. It comprises features known as the Table (the grassy plateau seen here), the Pinnacle and the Prison.

The 'Discovery' at Discovery Cove, Dundee. The ship was built to take Captain Scott to Antarctica.

The National Wallace Monument at Stirling was erected in the mid-19th century to commemorate William Wallace (c1270–1305), a hero of the struggle to free Scotland from English rule.

An entrant in the World Pipe Band championship, held every year in Glasgow.

The River Ba with the Black Mount beyond in the Central Highlands.

Tartan ties for sale in Edinburgh. The earliest known tartan in Scotland dates from the 3rd or 4th century, but it was not until the early 1800s that clans began adopting specific patterns and colours as their own.

Jedburgh Abbey, in the Borders, was founded in the 12th century.
Opposite: Buachaille Etive Beag reflected in Lochan na Fola, at the head of Glen Coe.

The extensive remains of Dirleton Castle, just north of North Berwick, in Lothian. It was destroyed by Oliver Cromwell in the mid-17th century.

The Heart of Midlothian was the nickname given to the old Tolbooth prison on Edinburgh's Royal Mile, just to the west of St Giles Kirk; this pattern on the cobbles marks the prison entrance.

Morar's white-sand beach is known as the 'Silver Sands'. The village lies on the Road to the Isles, which connects Fort William and Mallaig.

Robert the Bruce, one of Scotland's greatest heroes. This bronze statue of him overlooks the site of his famous victory at Bannockburn, outside Stirling, in 1314.

The Forth Bridge was designed to carry two rail tracks over the Firth of Forth between South Queensferry
and North Queensferry. It took seven years to build and was opened in 1890.
Opposite: birch and oak woodland surrounds Loch Ard, in the heart of the Trossachs.

The jagged gabbro peaks of the Black Cuillins beyond the Old Road Bridge over the River Sligachan on the Isle of Skye. The granite Red Cuillins are more rounded.

The icy summit of Buachaille Etive Beag, which means the little Shepherd of Etive, near the head of Glen Coe. It forms a twin with Buachaille Etive Mor (the Great Shepherd).

Loch Katrine in the Trossachs, seen from Ben A'an. Scottish novelist and poet Sir Walter Scott immortalised the lake in his epic poem 'The Lady of the Lake' (1810).

The Burn of Sorrow as it flows through Windy Pass in Dollar Glen, Clackmannanshire.

The ruins of St Andrew's Cathedral, built around 1160. It was destroyed during the Reformation, the religious conflict that took place between Catholics and Protestants in the 16th century.
Opposite: the view towards Arrochar Alps on the northern shores of Loch Lomond.

Brodick Castle, which stands at the foot of Goatfell Mountain just outside the main port of Brodick on the Isle of Arran. The site has been occupied by a stronghold of some kind since an Irish tribe settled on the island in the 5th century.

The Black Cuillins rising up from Loch Brittle, a sea loch on the west coast of Skye. The island is the largest of the Inner Hebrides.

*Corpach Basin at Fort William, the southern end of the Caledonian Canal, which stretches
60 miles (96km) up to Inverness by connecting a series of lochs in the Great Glen. Queen Victoria was
one of the first tourists to travel on the canal after its completion in 1822.*

The luxury Balmoral Hotel in central Edinburgh, seen from Calton Hill. With its 190ft (58m) tower, the Edwardian landmark is known as 'the grand old lady' of Princes Street.

Gearannan on the Isle of Lewis is a restored crofting village where cottages are now let as holiday accommodation. The last villagers moved out in 1974, leaving the settlement derelict for several years.

Impossibly romantic Eilean Donan Castle, on the west coast, stands on a rocky promontory between three lochs — Long, Duich and Alsh. It was once inhabited by the religious hermit St Donan, hence the name, which means Island of Donan.

The pinnacle rock stack known as the Old Man of Hoy lies off the coast of Hoy, in Orkney.
Opposite: the Glenfinnan monument on Loch Shiel, where Bonnie Prince Charlie raised the Jacobite standard in
1745 and rallied his clansmen to battle.

Ben Lomond beyond Loch Lomond, the largest inland area of water in Britain.

A lily-covered lochan on the Sutherland Moor, Argyll and Bute.

The golden sands at Coldbackie, which lies at the head of the Kyle of Tongue on the north coast of Sutherland.

The Italian Chapel on Lamb Holm, one of the smaller Orkney islands. It was created from two Nissen huts in World War II by Italian prisoners of war working on the Churchill Barriers.

The ruined tower of Ardvreck Castle, on Loch Assynt, Sutherland.
Opposite: the parallel 'roads' visible in Glen Roy, near the Great Glen, are the remnant shorelines of a glacial lake.

Ben Nevis, seen from across Loch Linnhe. The 'Ben', Britain's highest mountain (4,406ft / 1,344m), is known for its changeable and often unpleasant weather conditions.

Hermitage Castle, near Castleton, was an important stronghold during the Border wars and skirmishes that raged through the 14th to the 16th centuries. Feuding families were called Reivers.

On top of Ciste Dhubh, with views across Kintail, opposite the Isle of Skye. The peak is one of four Munros on a ridge known as the North Glen Shiel Range.

Ben Nevis from Banavie.

Robert Burns, on the High Street in Dumfries. 'Scotland's Bard' (born in 1759) died aged 37.

Autumn colour on the shores of Loch Katrine, in the Trossachs.

Crail's sheltered harbour, in eastern Fife. The straight arm of the breakwater was built in 1826 by Robert Stevenson, but the curved wall dates back to the 16th century.

The Scott Monument in Edinburgh's Princes Street commemorates Sir Walter Scott, who died in 1832.

Traditional Scotland: tartan and bagpipes at the Pitlochry Highland Games.

Inveraray, set on the shore of Loch Fyne, in Argyll. The 3rd Duke of Argyll built the town in the mid-18th century on the site of a former fishing village, rehousing the inhabitants on Main Street.

Glasgow University, Scotland's second oldest university after St Andrew's.
Opposite: Rannoch Moor seen from Glencoe.

Beechwoods near the village of Glencoe. This is one of the few pockets of deciduous woodland in the glen.

The Commando Memorial by Scott Sutherland, near the World War II training grounds at Spean Bridge.

Glen Coe from the pass, with the outcrops on Bidean Nam Bian known as the Three Sisters on the left.

The Victorian town of Oban, with views beyond the island of Kerrera across to Mull. It has been a main communications point since the arrival of the railway and the development of steamships.

The Pitlochry Hydro Hotel. One of the main attractions in the town is the Pitlochry Dam,
which created Loch Faskally.

View across the River Tay at Perth. The town was an important ecclesiastical, commercial and administrative hub during the Middle Ages, and a cotton-manufacturing centre in the 19th century.

The cloisters of the abbey on Iona, off the west coast of Mull. After centuries of disuse, the complex was restored in the 1930s and now offers retreats and welcomes visitors.

The George Hutcheson Statue next to the City Chambers, Glasgow.

The beautiful walled garden at Crathes Castle, southwest of Aberdeen, is divided into eight themed areas.
It was created in the 20th century in the grounds of the 16th-century castle.

Plockton, on a sheltered bay at the seaward end of Loch Carron in the Highlands. Formerly a fishing and crofting village, it now attracts artists and holidaymakers.

The tower of the former Luma Light Bulb Factory, in Glasgow, once used to test lightbulbs. One of the few modernist buildings in the city, it was completed in 1938.

The small town of Dunkeld, beside the River Tay in Perthshire.

Dunskey Castle, now a romatic clifftop ruin, above Portpatrick in Dumfires and Galloway. It looks across the Irish Channel to Donaghdee.

A window in the wall of Claypots Castle, on the outskirts of Dundee. The building is a good example of a Z-plan tower house – a rectangular block with round towers at two of the diagonally opposite corners.

Part of the Cameron Memorial Fountain in the Charing Cross area of Glasgow. Sir Charles Cameron
(1841–1925) was a newspaper editor and politician.

The Hills of Hoy across Hoy Sound, Orkney. The island takes its name from the
Old Norse word 'Haey', meaning high.

The Acropolis on Calton Hill, Edinburgh. Begun in 1822 as a replica of the Parthenon in Athens, it was meant to commemorate those who died in the Napoleonic Wars but was never completed.
Opposite: fireworks light up the capital's skyline.